Who's Who in the Zoo?
Dot-to-Dot Fun

Barbara Soloff Levy

DOVER PUBLICATIONS, INC.
Mineola, New York

Note

If you go to a zoo, you will see animals such as lions and elephants—animals you won't see anywhere else! By the time you get to the end of this entertaining dot-to-dot book, you will have encountered a koala, a llama, a rhinoceros, a polar bear, a wolf, and 25 other fascinating creatures!

First, read the hint below each dot-to-dot puzzle. Try to figure out what you will see when the picture is complete. Then, using a pencil, begin at dot 1 and draw a line to dot 2. Next, draw a line from dot 2 to dot 3, and so on, in number order. When you have connected all of the dots, you will see your picture! At the back of the book is a list of what you will find in the puzzles, just in case.

Are you ready to have some dot-to-dot fun? Get your pencil out and let's go to the zoo!

Bibliographical Note

Who's Who in the Zoo? Dot-to-Dot Fun is a new work, first published by Dover Publications, Inc., in 2007.

DOVER *Pictorial Archive* SERIES

This book belongs to the Dover Pictorial Archive Series. You may use the designs and illustrations for graphics and crafts applications, free and without special permission, provided that you include no more than four in the same publication or project. (For permission for additional use, please write to Permissions Department, Dover Publications, Inc., 31 East 2nd Street, Mineola, N.Y. 11501.)

However, republication or reproduction of any illustration by any other graphic service, whether it be in a book or in any other design resource, is strictly prohibited.

International Standard Book Number
ISBN-13: 978-0-486-46181-6
ISBN-10: 0-486-46181-5

Manufactured in the United States of America
Dover Publications, Inc., 31 East 2nd Street, Mineola, N.Y. 11501

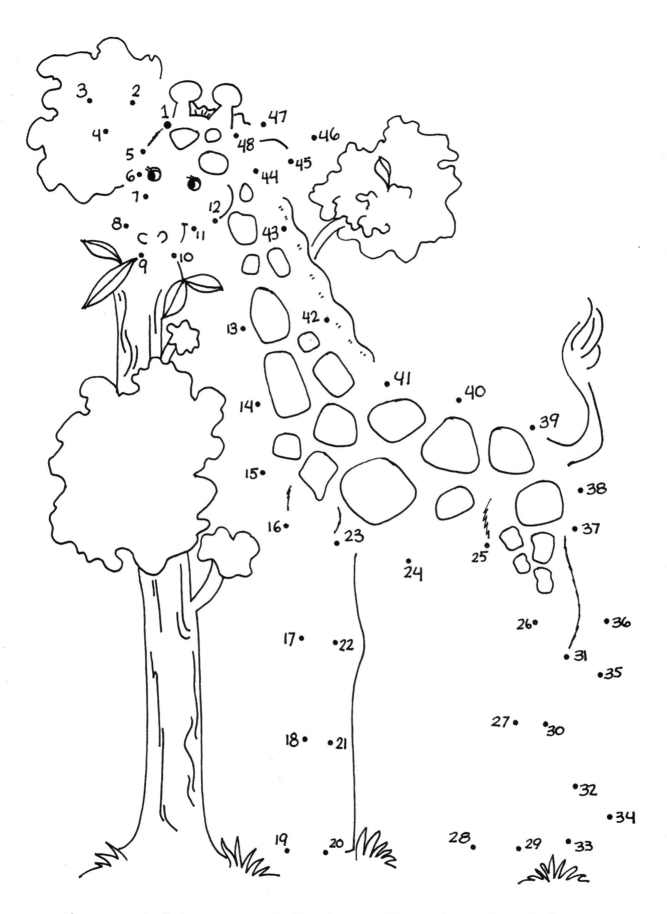

I am so tall, I can reach the tops of trees to eat tasty leaves.
Connect the dots to see my picture.

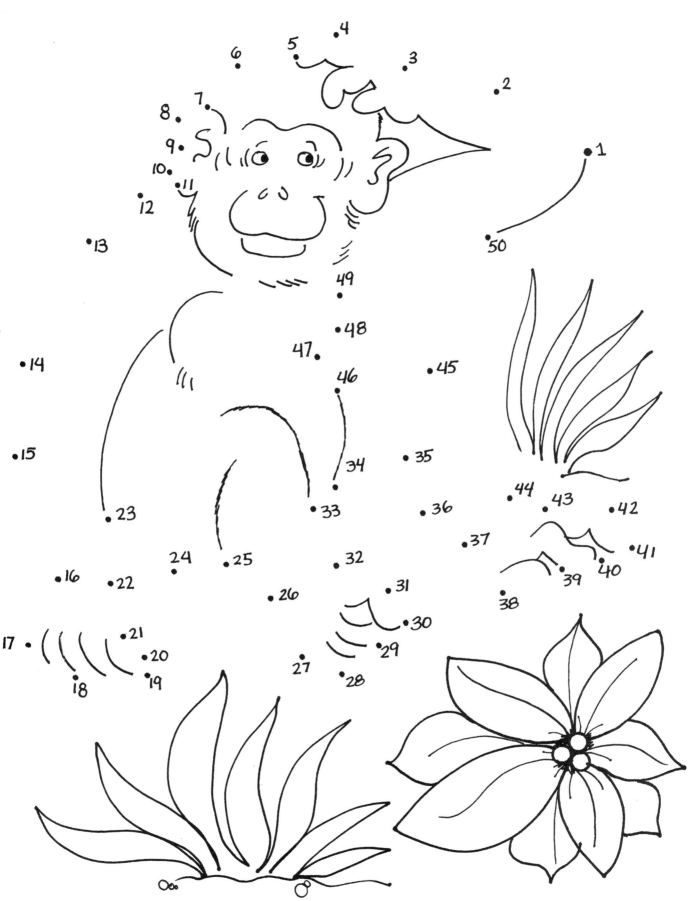

Scientists can "speak" to me using simple sign language.
Follow the dots to find out who I am.

I carry my baby around in a pouch.
Find out who I am by connecting the dots.

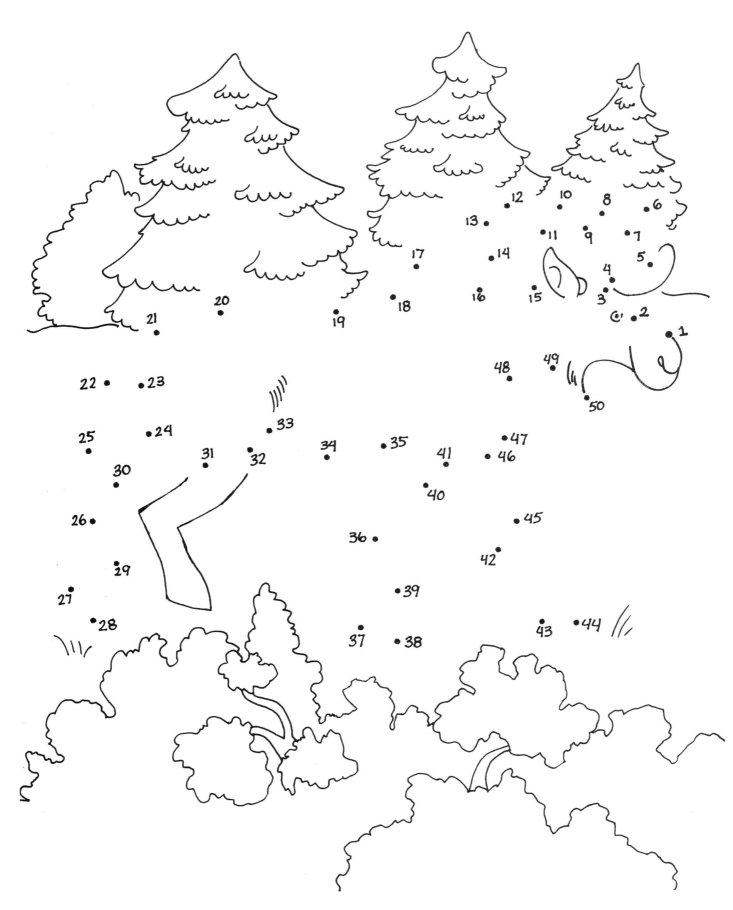

The cold northern forests are where I make my home.
Follow the dots to see my picture.

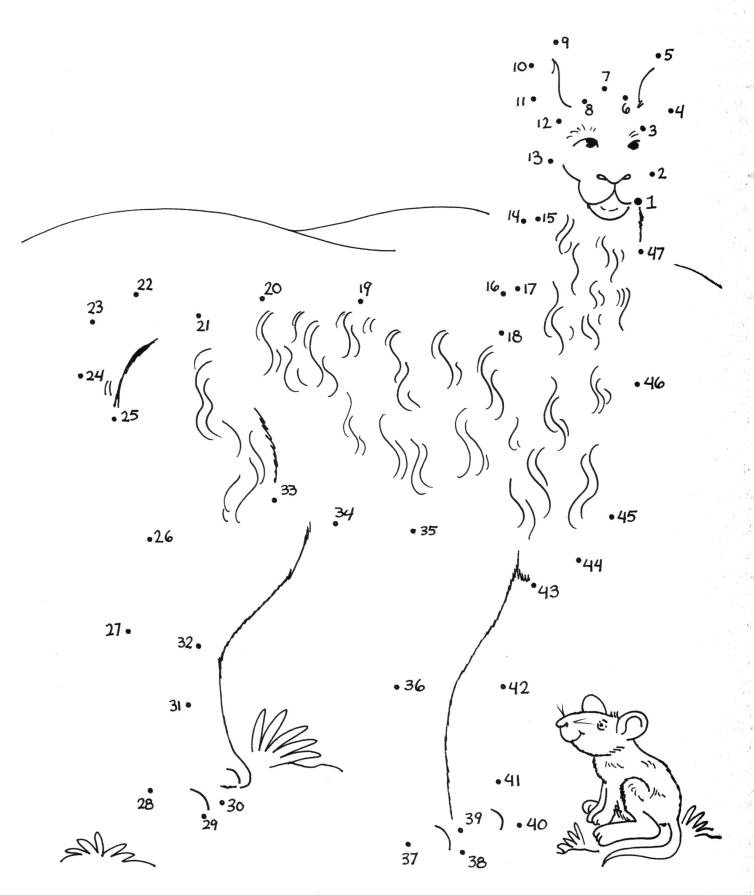

I am a large, sure-footed animal that can carry heavy loads.
To see my picture, just connect the dots!

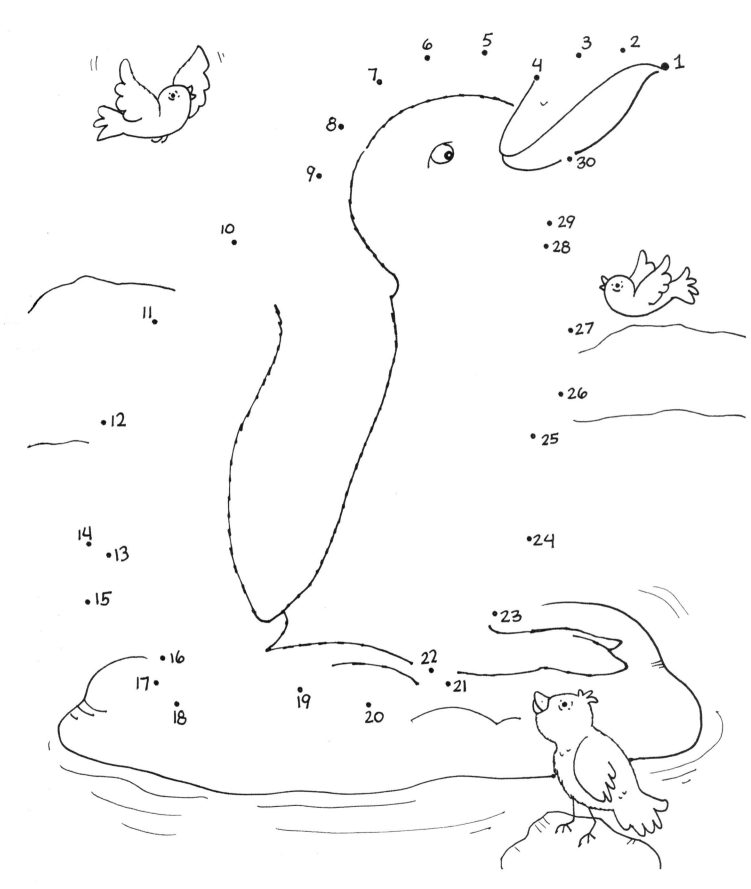

I'm a black-and-white bird that loves to swim in an icy pond.
Follow the dots and there I am!

Look out! I might be slithering along the ground.
Connect the dots to see what I look like.

I am a large cat that is known as the "king of beasts."
Follow the dots to find out who I am.

You may find me swinging from branch to branch in the trees.
To see my picture, connect the dots.

When I'm on the ground, I walk on my knuckles.
Follow the dots and I'm sure you'll recognize me!

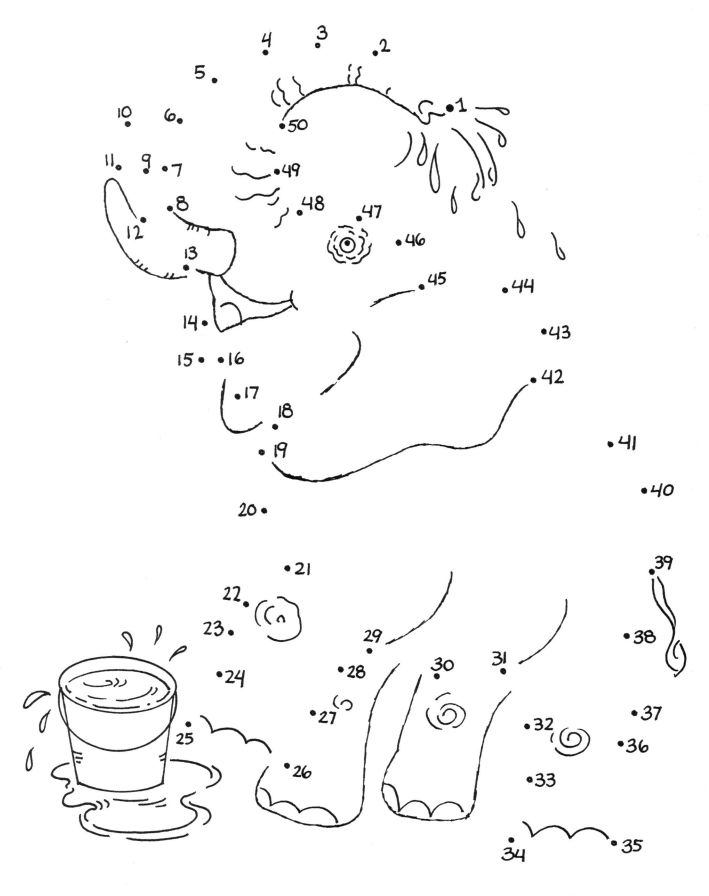

I am the largest animal in the zoo. Of course, you know who I am, but follow the dots anyway to see me.

I am a tall bird that may weigh over three hundred pounds!
To see me, just connect the dots.

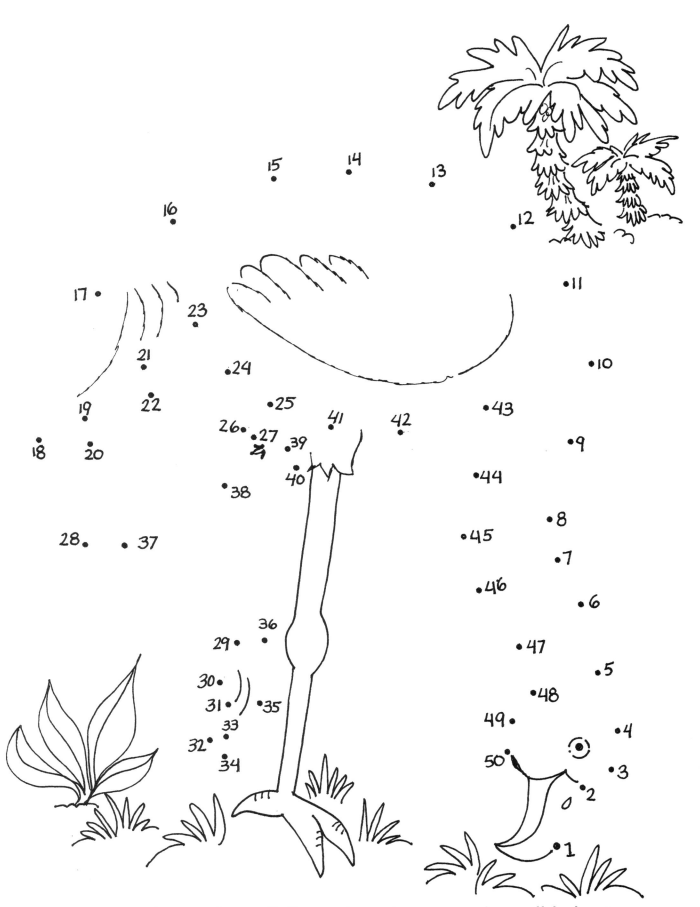

It's easy for me to walk through water on my long, thin legs.
If you connect the dots, you will find out who I am.

My enormous body is covered with a thick "hide," or skin.
Follow the dots to see my picture.

I am a type of large parrot. I have a feathered crest on my head.
You can see me by connecting the dots.

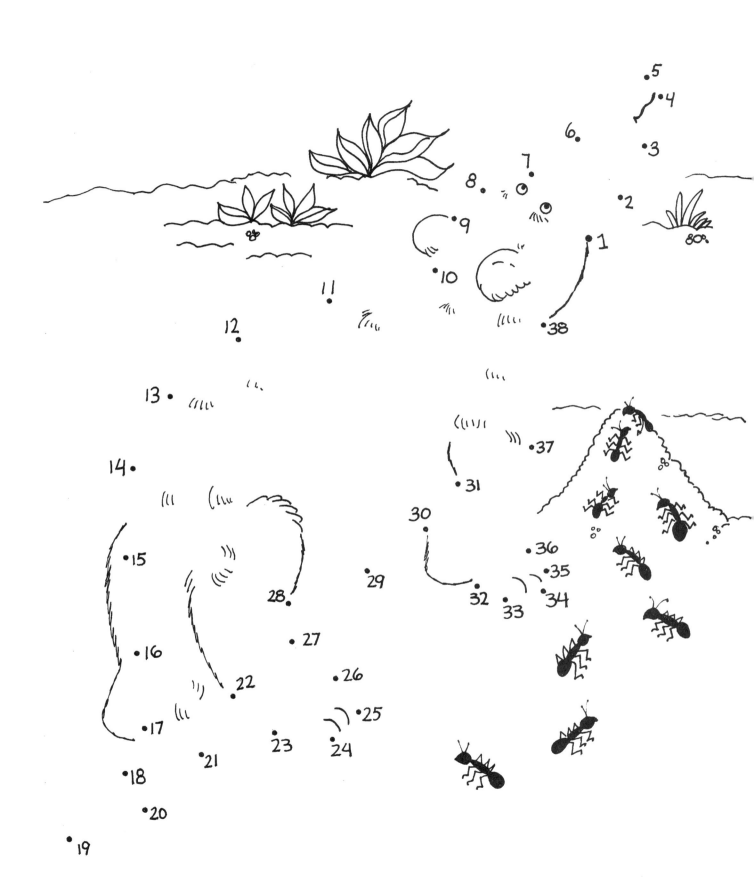

My long snout is handy for digging up ants to eat.
To see what I look like, follow the dots.

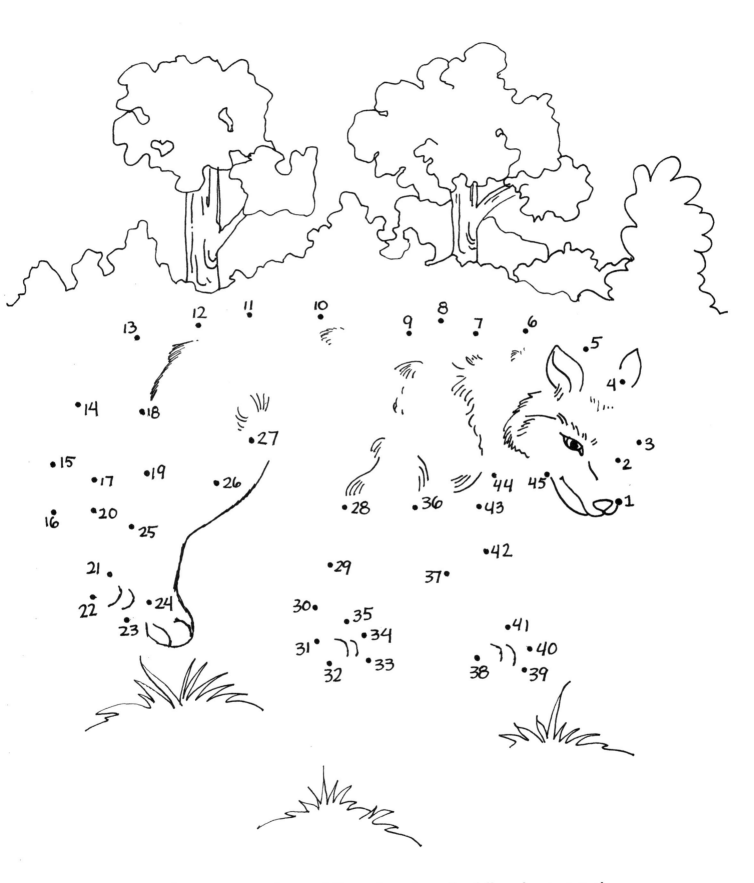

I'm a large member of the dog family. I live in a pack.
Connect the dots to see me.

17

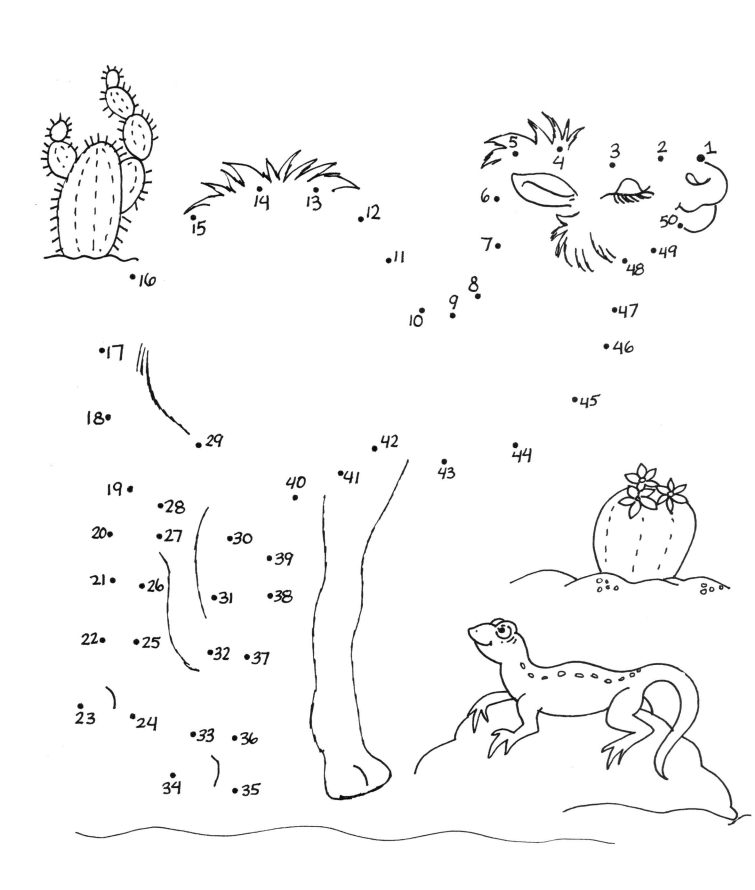

I can go without water for a very long time.
Follow the dots to find out who I am.

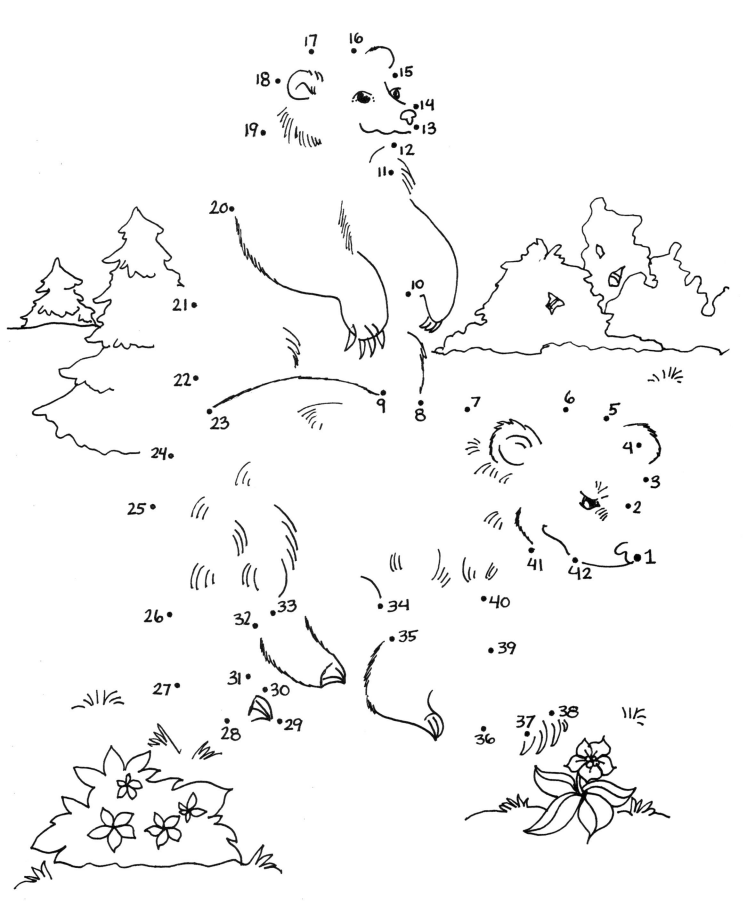

Our large teeth and thick brown fur make us easy to recognize.
Connect the dots to see our picture.

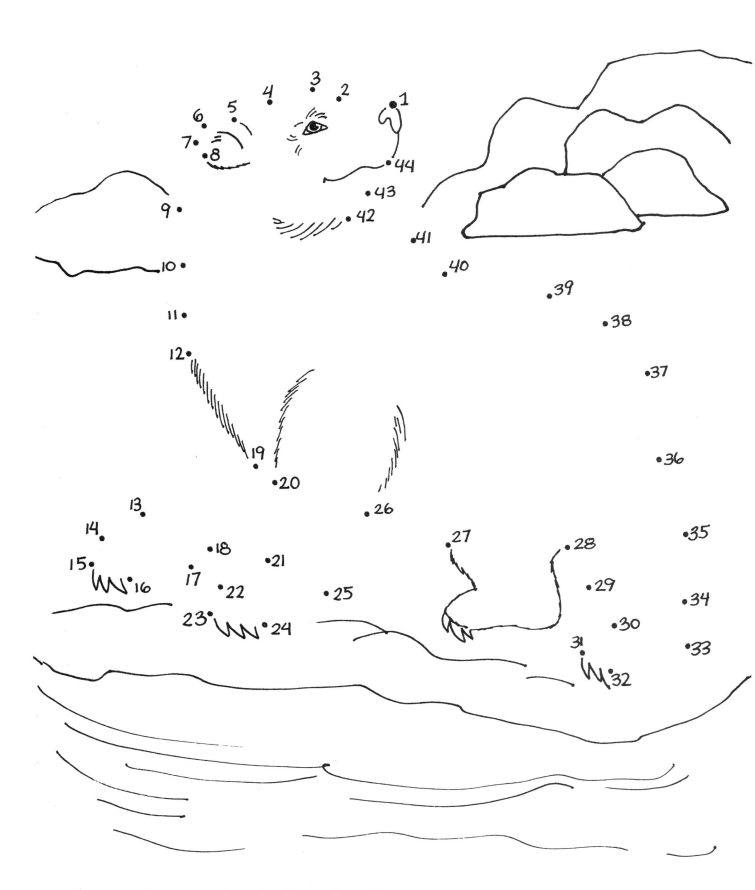

I am a large animal with yellowish-white fur that lives in the far north.
See my picture by following the dots.

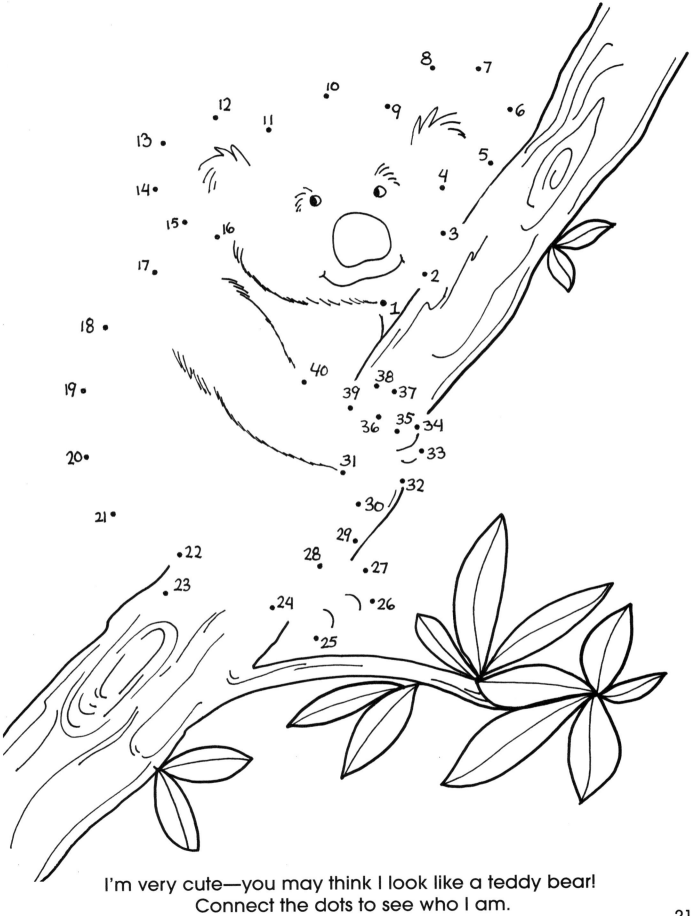

I'm very cute—you may think I look like a teddy bear!
Connect the dots to see who I am.

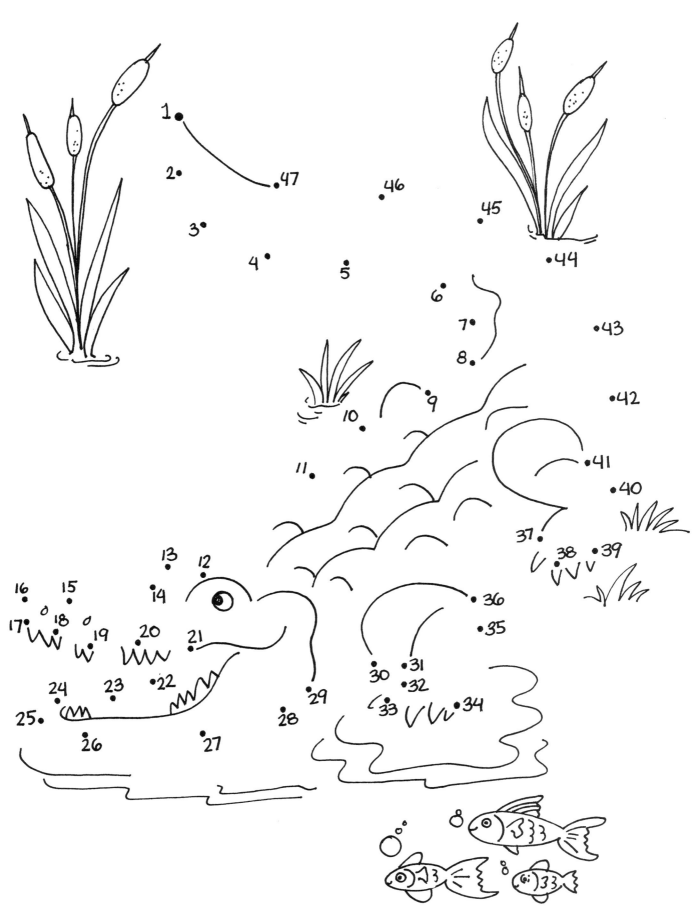

I am a water animal that has a long jaw filled with sharp teeth.
To see me, just follow the dots.

I am a type of cattle whose body is covered with thick brown fur.
You can see what I look like by connecting the dots.

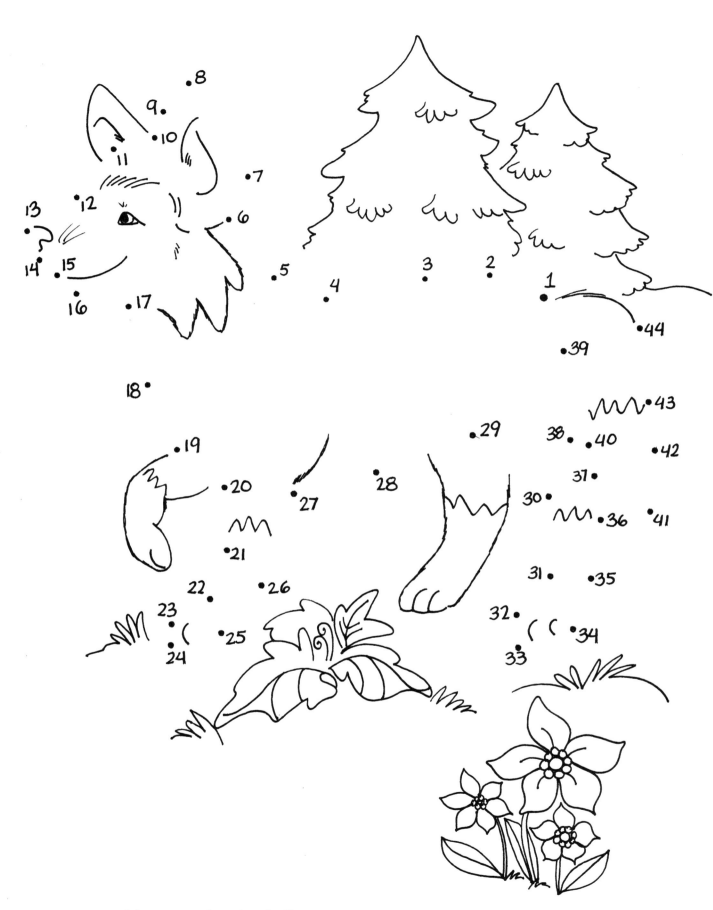

I have a bushy tail, and I might remind you of a wolf.
Follow the dots to see who I am.

When you see the dark spots on my fur,
you will know what type of big cat I am.

I'm a big cat whose stripes make me easy to recognize at the zoo.
Who am I? Connect the dots to find out!

My large wings and claws make me a very powerful bird.
Follow the dots and you will see who I am.

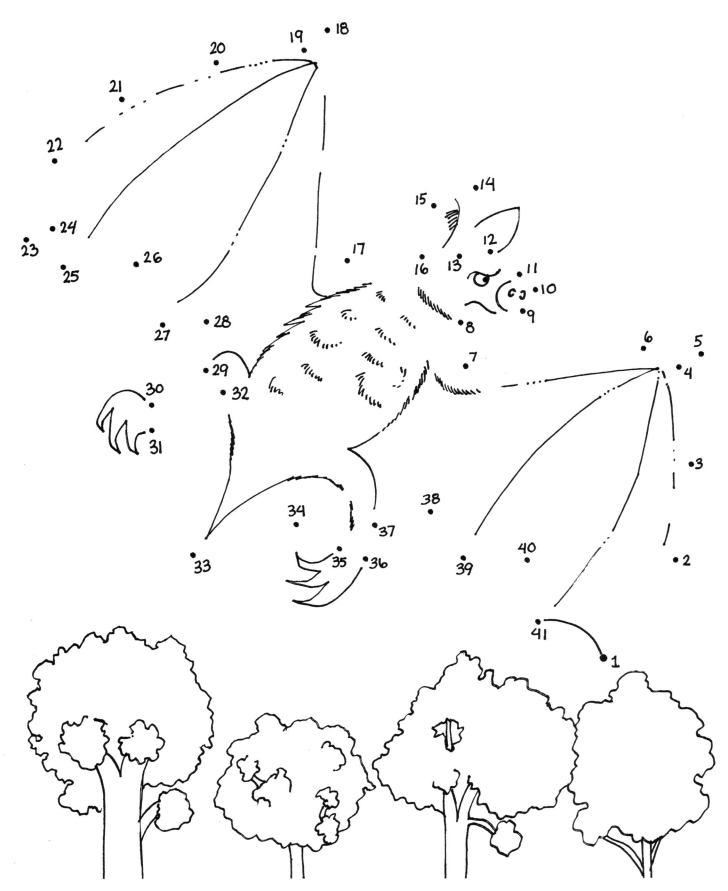

I am a small flying animal that is most active at night.
To find out who I am, connect the dots.

As long as I have bamboo to chew on, I am happy!
Just follow the dots and you will see my picture.

I am a type of wild horse that is known for its stripes.
Connect the dots to find out who I am.